FSC
www.fsc.org
MIX
Paper from
responsible sources
FSC® C109093

THIS IS A CARLTON BOOK

Published by Carlton Books Ltd
20 Mortimer Street
London W1T 3JW

Text Copyright © 2019 Carlton Books
Design Copyright © 2019 Carlton Books Limited

All screenshots and images of Apex Legends characters/gameplay
© 2019 Electronic Arts Inc.
© 2019 Respawn Entertainment Trademarks belong to their
respective owners. All rights reserved.

ISBN 978-1-78739-354-7

Project Editor: Ross Hamilton
Author: Dom Peppiatt
Art Editor: Russell Knowles
Design: Harriet Knight
Production: Rachel Burgess

A CIP catalogue for this book is available from the British Library

10 9 8 7 6 5 4 3 2 1

Printed in China

THE CHAMPION'S GUIDE TO APEX LEGENDS

EVERYTHING YOU NEED TO DOMINATE THE BATTLE ROYALE

CARLTON
BOOKS

CONTENTS

CLASS BREAKDOWN

10 THINGS TO KNOW

WELCOME TO APEX LEGENDS – THE NEWEST HIT GAME FROM RESPAWN ENTERTAINMENT. HERE'S THE MOST VITAL INFORMATION YOU NEED TO KNOW ABOUT THE GAME.

1 WHAT IS APEX LEGENDS?

Apex Legends is a first-person shooter, squad-based Battle Royale game with Hero Shooter elements designed for Xbox One, PC and PS4 that anyone can play absolutely for free.

2 THE NEXT EVOLUTION OF BATTLE ROYALE

Show 'em what you're made of in Apex Legends, a free-to-play Battle Royale game where contenders from across the Frontier team up to battle for glory, fame, and fortune.

WHAT IS A BATTLE ROYALE?

Battle Royales are competitive games that pit up to 100 players against each other in a last-man-standing firefight. The map shrinks, bringing players closer to each other as time runs out.

3 WHAT MAKES APEX LEGENDS DIFFERENT?

Apex Legends introduces Legends into the genre: individual characters that have unique traits and abilities that allow them to dominate the battlefield in different ways. You are also put in groups, battling to be the best of 60 players.

4 WHO MADE APEX LEGENDS?

Apex Legends is made by Respawn Entertainment. The developer also made Titanfall and Titanfall 2, and is currently working on a Star Wars game, too. The studio is known for fast, movement-focused FPS games, and was founded by ex-Call of Duty developers.

5

HOW MUCH DOES IT COST?

Apex Legends has been – and always will be – free. The game is a free-to-play title, supported by microtransactions that come in the form of Apex Coins. These coins can be exchanged for Apex Packs (which contain cosmetic items), but the base game will never cost a penny.

6

WHERE CAN I PLAY IT?

Apex Legends is available to download digitally on the Xbox One, PlayStation 4 and PC (via Origin). You will need an active internet connection play, since everything in this game takes place online. There is no solo offline mode.

7

16
www.pegi.info

TEEN T ® CONTENT RATED BY ESRB

WHAT MATURITY RATING IS THIS GAME?

The ERSB rates Apex Legends as 13 and older via the Teen rating in the US, and comes with a PEGI 16 rating in the UK. The Finisher moves are the closest to real violence the game gets, but otherwise there is no blood or gore or crude language.

8

HOW MANY CHARACTERS ARE THERE?

At the time of writing, there are nine playable characters in Apex Legends: Bangalore, Bloodhound, Caustic, Gibraltar, Lifeline, Mirage, Octane, Pathfinder and Wraith. But Respawn plans to add more characters all the time.

9

HOW DO I GET BETTER AT THE GAME?

Time, patience and dedication! But there are many skills you can learn that will help you master the game and get the advantage over other players – hopefully this book can help you learn some of the most important tricks.

10

I'M NEW — AM I TOO LATE TO THE GAME?

Not at all! Apex Legends continues to grow and add new players all the time. The matchmaking system in the game seems to connect players of all skill levels into matches even today – there's no better time to start playing.

LEARN THE BASICS

APEX LEGENDS MAY SEEM LIKE A SIMPLE GAME, BUT THERE ARE A SERIES OF RULES YOU NEED TO KNOW BEFORE YOU START PLAYING.

THE BASICS

Each Apex Legends game consists of up to 60 players, working together in teams of three. There are a maximum of 20 teams in every game, though this may be lower, depending on the matchmaking process.

Players have 100 health, and can reduce damage taken by picking up armour or helmets. You will be knocked down out if you take 100 damage to your health, and you will be killed if you take 50 damage while knocked down.

You can be revived by teammates when knocked down, and you can be respawned by teammates after being killed. If your teammates fail to revive or respawn you within the time limit, you will be eliminated. If all three members of your team are killed, your team is eliminated from the game.

You deal damage with weapons, which can be picked up from the ground, loot bins, or other players. Each weapon will need to be upgraded with attachments you can find in the map.

DON'T CHEAT!

Respawn and EA has already banned 35,000 players from playing Apex Legends – and that number is rising all the time. On PC, players can install illicit software that allows them to see through walls, aim automatically and slow down other players. This software is not supported by the developers, and is easily detected. Using it could result in your IP address and hardware being banned forever.

ROUNDS

Apex Legends matches are split into Rounds. You can tell which Round you're in because the announcer will say it, or you'll see it under your minimap. There are a maximum of eight rounds in each match: some broken up with Wait and Closing periods. Wait shows you where the map will close to, and Closing forces you to move in.

Anyone outside the Ring will suffer Health damage every 1.5 seconds, the amount of which changes each Round. The longer the game goes on, the less of the map is playable, reducing by up to 1115m per Round.

WINNING

The last team standing will win the game. It is possible to win the game when knocked down or killed, if your team makes it to the end of the game.

The winning team will receive bonus XP at the end of the game – even if one or two members have been killed. You will not receive XP if you leave the game once you're knocked down or killed.

HEADS UP

TO BE VICTORIOUS AT APEX LEGENDS, YOU HAVE TO UNDERSTAND WHAT YOU'RE LOOKING AT ON-SCREEN, AND HOW TO PLAY.

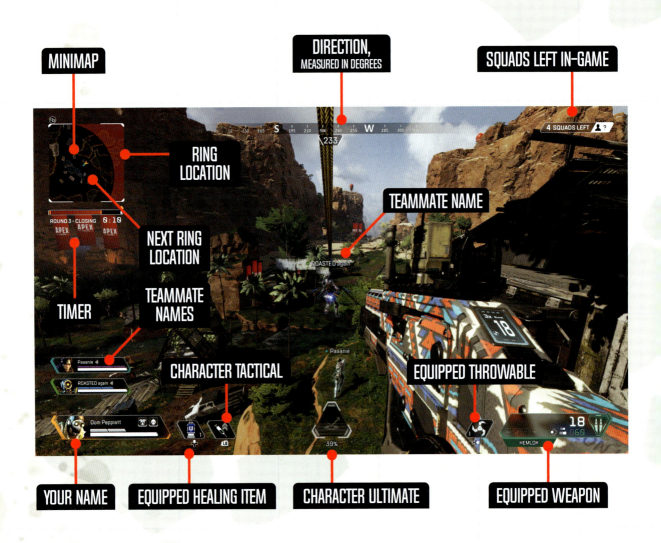

MINIMAP

DIRECTION, MEASURED IN DEGREES

SQUADS LEFT IN-GAME

RING LOCATION

TEAMMATE NAME

NEXT RING LOCATION

TIMER

TEAMMATE NAMES

CHARACTER TACTICAL

EQUIPPED THROWABLE

YOUR NAME

EQUIPPED HEALING ITEM

CHARACTER ULTIMATE

EQUIPPED WEAPON

IN CONTROL

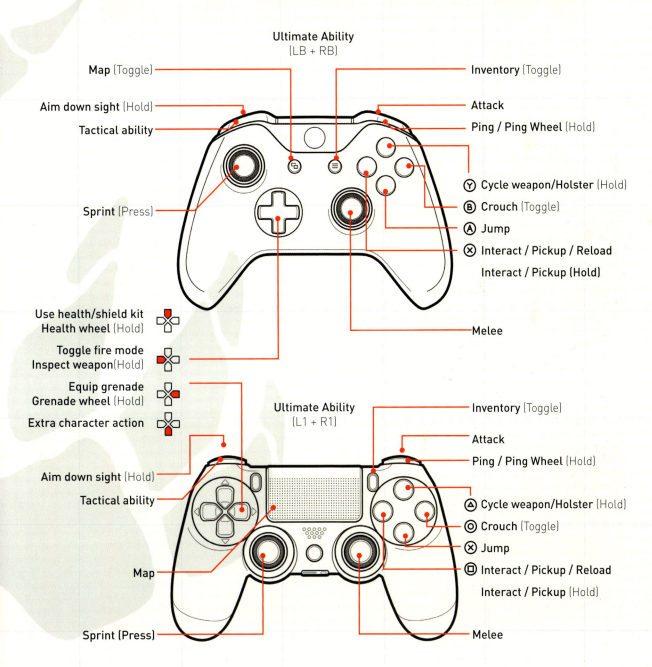

Ultimate Ability
(LB + RB)

Map (Toggle)

Aim down sight (Hold)

Tactical ability

Sprint (Press)

Inventory (Toggle)

Attack

Ping / Ping Wheel (Hold)

Ⓨ Cycle weapon/Holster (Hold)
Ⓑ Crouch (Toggle)
Ⓐ Jump
Ⓧ Interact / Pickup / Reload
Interact / Pickup (Hold)

Melee

Use health/shield kit
Health wheel (Hold)

Toggle fire mode
Inspect weapon (Hold)

Equip grenade
Grenade wheel (Hold)

Extra character action

Ultimate Ability
(L1 + R1)

Inventory (Toggle)

Attack

Ping / Ping Wheel (Hold)

Aim down sight (Hold)

Tactical ability

△ Cycle weapon/Holster (Hold)
◎ Crouch (Toggle)
⨯ Jump
▢ Interact / Pickup / Reload
Interact / Pickup (Hold)

Map

Sprint (Press)

Melee

TERMS OF ENGAGEMENT

USE THIS GLOSSARY TO GET TO KNOW APEX LEGENDS' KEY ELEMENTS.

DEATH BOXES

The boxes enemies leave behind once they've been eliminated, full of all the loot they found.

RESPAWN BEACON

Identified with a green light, these machines will call your allies back into the map via a dropship.

LOOT TICK

Small (but valuable!) robots that like to hide around the map. Listen for their beeping: they drop great loot!

PING

An action that notifies allies of a point of interest: an enemy, item, location, death box, or downed ally.

RING

The moving wall that determines the game area. Stay inside it, or you'll begin to take damage.

HOT ZONE

The best place to land in the early game. This area is usually hotly contested but offers great rewards.

ABILITIES

Each of the playable characters in the game has three unique abilities: a passive, a tactical and an ultimate.

KNOCKED

The term for when you get taken down – losing your 100 health – but before you get killed. Vulnerable to finishers.

CHAMPION

The player with the most kills in the game. Take out a Champion for bonus 500XP at the end of your game.

LOOT

The term for any item that can be picked up. Each piece of loot has a level: Common, Rare, Legendary or Epic.

KING'S CANYON

APEX LEGENDS' MAP IS A WILD AND VARIED LANDSCAPE. HERE'S EVERYTHING YOU NEED TO KNOW TO TAME IT.

Apex Legends was built to be a fast, mobile game played in squads of three. It sounds obvious, but keep that in mind while exploring: always move.

KEY LOCATIONS

Most guns and abilities are designed to work best at mid- or close-range – don't take potshots across the map at well-fortified enemies: you'll just give yourself away!

ARTILLERY

Though ziplines connect the three large buildings – making it a quick place to loot – Artillery is massively popular as a landing zone, meaning you usually have to fight off a few teams to take advantage of the good loot.

RELAY

Relay is positioned ideally for teams that like to raid and run, and rarely has many people dead set on exploring it. It's good for quick raids, but thanks to its mix of high and low ground, it's not a great place to stick around.

AIRBASE

If you're a daredevil, this one's for you: two massive, exposed runways (connected with a zipline) are home to good loot... but be aware that you're always likely to be in someone's sights out here.

SWAMPS

The largest amount of loot in one place, Swamps is a great landing location both for the number of things you can find and the size of the zone. Escaping is tricky though, thanks to how low Swamps sits on the map.

KEY LOCATIONS CONTINUED

You can climb doors: open one, and wall-climb on top of it. This can be a handy way of surprising raiding teams or getting the jump on unsuspecting players.

THUNDERDOME

A great location for dynamic firefights between the suspended cages and rocks, this location is home to a handy Respawn Beacon and some good loot spread across the various interconnect levels.

BUNKER

An intense, awkward central corridor often houses good loot, and almost always ends in a collision with another team. Good projectile users flourish here – just watch out for Caustic mains and ambushes behind doors.

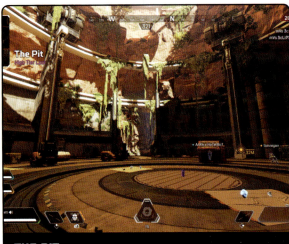

THE PIT

Thanks to how secluded it is, The Pit looks tempting at first, but be warned: there's no cover, and enemies can get the jump on you from three entry points. Loot Ticks like it here, but so do roving enemy teams.

SKULL TOWN

One of the busiest drop zones thanks to its central location, a smart player aims for the rooftops here: get a gun, pick off weak players, stay indoors and heal up. Don't stick around and get trapped.

WETLANDS

It's quick to raid the dozen or so buildings that make up the Wetlands, then you can focus on pushing through the easily defended choke point to Artillery. Even non-Pathfinder players can command the rooftops here.

WATCHTOWER NORTH

With the nearest Respawn Beacon located in Cascades, you know you've got a fight on your hands if you're knocked down here. Don't worry though – a good vantage point and decent amounts of loot make for a solid area.

RUNOFF

If you land in Runoff – and live – you'll come away all geared up. Thanks to the massive amount of loot here, it's a hotspot... and there are no Respawn Beacons handily placed. A high risk, high reward zone.

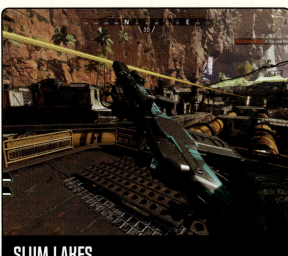

SLUM LAKES

A fairly popular landing zone, this knot of small buildings has a lot of loot, but you're unlikely to find much high-level gear. From here, if you fancy a scrap, head to Runoff or The Pit.

THE JUMP

THE JUMP IS WHERE IT ALL BEGINS – WHERE LEGENDS ARE BORN. MAKE SURE YOU KNOW HOW TO GET THE FIRST STEPS OF YOUR JOURNEY RIGHT.

Apex Legends is all about surviving for as long as possible – and that means nailing your landing and starting your game off right. Are you a dive-bomber or a glider? Did you know that you can taper off your initial free-fall into a more controlled glide once you get full control over your character? Have you ever been the victim of a jumpmaster bonking you away from your teammates on a big red balloon (and do you want to make sure that never happens again?). Then read on to discover some essential tips behind the perfect jump.

DO
Keep an eye out for other player's contrails: these are the best visual indicators of where other players are going to land. If you see lots of colours mingling together, you might want to keep your distance.

DON'T
Assume the Jump ends when you near the ground: you can maintain the momentum from your fall even when you approach King's Canyon, meaning skilled players can launch themselves even further with enough practice.

DON'T Let the Jumpmaster do all the work. When you near the landing zone, make sure to split off from your boss early – stick close, but peel off. This way, you're not fighting for loot and taking each other's things.

DO Listen to your friends' suggestions: if you're playing with randoms, they may have a lot of experience in one area if they're pinging it over and over again. Have confidence in your choices, but remember to work as a team!

DON'T Abandon your teammates. This game is designed for three players and you'll notice Apex Legends is a very unforgiving experience if you hightail it to the other end of the map without your friends. Solo players don't get respawned.

DO Take note of the blue circle on your map, which is called a 'hot zone' – you get extra XP for killing enemies here and there are higher levels of loot when you land... just be aware it's a very popular destination.

DON'T Bully randoms. Say you're in a team of two and you – for fun – decide to bonk the third player against a building or balloon... This may seem like harmless fun, but you're ruining someone's experience (and players have been banned for less).

DO Measure your trajectory: the white bars represent your altitude (height) and velocity (speed). Mastering the angle of descent is key to getting where you want to go quicker than other players.

Respawn Beacon
Bring banner to revive dead squad members.

Supply Ship
High tier loot barge.

Hot Zone
High tier loot zone. Chance for a fully kitted weapon.

Supply Drop
Chance for high tier loot.

CLASS BREAKDOWN

BANGALORE

COCKY, CONFIDENT AND A CRACK SHOT, BANGALORE IS THE LAST PERSON YOU WANT TO FACE ON THE BATTLEFIELD.

Bangalore – real name Anita Williams – was born into a military family. Everyone (and everything) she knew growing up was IMC. Thanks to being raised in a ruthless, well-oiled military family, Bangalore has been proficient with just about every weapon going ever since she was a child.

Bangalore's mastery of the weapons she uses is legendary: she can take apart a gun and put it back together in seconds. Blindfolded. She's a real pro. Three years ago, Bangalore and her brother went on a mission for the IMC, tasked with fetching a mercenary fleet from the Outlands in order to recruit them against the Militia.

It seems her mission was a trap, though, and she was separated from her brother. Now alone, and harbouring a deadly grudge, Bangalore fights in the Apex Games in the hope of raising funds to get her back to her waiting family.

PASSIVE

DOUBLE TIME

Taking fire when Sprint is active will increase your speed by 30% for a short amount of time. Best used to accelerate to cover, or as a speed boost for returning fire.

TACTICAL

SMOKE LAUNCHER

A high-velocity smoke canister you can detonate to create a smoke wall. Handy for escaping enemies or suppressing unsuspecting teams.

ULTIMATE

ROLLING THUNDER

An artillery strike that peppers a large area with ballistic missiles, killing any downed players – friendly or hostile. Best used for large-scale fights or ambushes.

Bangalore is a great beginner character thanks to her traditional FPS setup. Newbies should start with her.

Be careful when combating Bloodhound players as a Bangalore: his Ultimate allows him to see through smoke, ruining the element of surprise.

Don't be shy about using Smoke Launcher: it has a low cooldown and lends itself to frequent, aggressive use.

BLOODHOUND

A MYSTERIOUS TRACKER WITH THE POWER OF GODS ON THEIR SIDE, BLOODHOUND IS AS FEARSOME AS THEY ARE UNPREDICTABLE.

Throughout the Outlands, people know Bloodhound as one of the greatest hunters in history. But despite their (in)famous status, people know practically nothing else about this mysterious prodigy: some say they're a former slave out for revenge, some say they talk to the Gods, some say they're a rich vigilante that happens to be half bat.

For all the hearsay, what's truly known of Bloodhound is this: they're lethal. Whispers suggest the technological tracker calls upon Earth's Norse Gods for aim in times of need, but no-one that's heard that for sure has lived to tell the tale. No-one even knows where Bloodhound came from, or what their real name is.

Bloodhound believes in fate – that everyone that meets them has already had their destiny predetermined... and that's probably true, because as soon as they know Bloodhound is near, they're as good as dead.

PASSIVE · TRACKER

Lets you see tracks left by your enemies – and how recently they were active. Very useful for predicting enemy movement and locking down a whole team's position.

TACTICAL · EYE OF THE ALLFATHER

Briefly reveal hidden enemies, traps, and clues in buildings and foliage in front of you. Use this to scope out new areas.

ULTIMATE · BEAST OF THE HUNT

Activating this ability may take a little while, but it gives a boost to your speed and highlights enemies. Use this speed to bear down on your foes.

Bloodhound comes into their own in choke points: fire up your Ultimate to put the pressure on and share the locations of enemy teams with your

Though Bloodhound's Ultimate normally takes a little while to rev up, activating it while climbing a wall readies it immediately.

Bloodhound players are big boons to the team – make sure you ping enemy tracks located via Tracker: your teammates can't see what you see!

30   NE   60   75   E   105

\ 59 /
Ring closing in:

3:26   ///

ROUND 2

Door Used (22m)
Age: 42 Sec.

CAUSTIC

A BRILLIANT, TWISTED MIND AND A MASTER OF TRAPS AND POISON ATTACKS, THIS LEGEND THRIVES ON THE ELEMENT OF SURPRISE.

Caustic's motives for entering the Apex Games are perhaps the most sinister of all the Legends. The man – once known as Alexander Nox – is a scientist with a hunger for experimentation. Once the bright young head scientist of a leading Frontier pesticide manufacturer, Nox became unhealthily obsessed with how his chemicals could eat away at anything they touched.

The once idealistic young scientist worked day and night on new formulas, turning from an eager young chemist into a twisted madman, experimenting on living tissues.

After alerting his bosses with his unethical experiments, Nox went missing – presumed dead. Humbert Labs burned to the ground and its employees were dead. Nox went dark, off the grid. However, a new competitor named Caustic soon started gaining notoriety in the Apex Games, eager to test lethal new chemical concoctions...

PASSIVE

NOX VISION

Allows you to see enemies through your gas – which is incredibly handy if you've detonated traps and thrown grenades into an enemy team's position.

TACTICAL

NOX GAS TRAP

Drop canisters that release deadly Nox gas when shot or triggered by enemies. The traps impair your opponents' vision and slow down their movement.

ULTIMATE

NOX GAS GRENADE

Blankets a large area in Nox gas: the best endgame tactical ability, as it can pollute most of the smallest game ring, affecting multiple enemies at once.

Thanks to enemies that trigger your traps becoming visible on your map, Caustic is a great tool for detecting an enemy presence early.

Be mindful of your positioning when using Caustic: his abilities hurt allies. Make sure to splinter off from your squad when engaging enemy positions.

Push when you have Ultimate. Caustic can be a real pain to escape from when his vision is active and you can't see or move very far.

GIBRALTAR

AS STURDY AS THE ROCK HE'S NAMED AFTER, GIBRALTAR IS — SOMETIMES LITERALLY — AN IMMOVABLE FORCE ON THE BATTLEFIELD.

Makoa Gibraltar – the 30-year-old gentle giant from the planet Solace – is the son of two Search and Rescue Association of Solace volunteers, and that shows in his personality. Gibraltar's main priority is getting others out of danger - something he learned the hard way when his father lost his arm saving him and his boyfriend from a mudslide.

After discovering a life of mischief wasn't for him, the big defender decided to look elsewhere for fulfilment. Gibraltar came to the Apex Games after seeing many of his friends and loved ones join the tournament in the hopes of cashing in – but getting badly hurt in the process. Now, he plays in the games with the express motivation of putting himself in the line of fire in order to protect them, putting his rebellious nature and good heart to work.

PASSIVE — GUN SHIELD

Aiming down sights deploys a gun shield that blocks incoming fire. This makes Gibraltar the best tank in the game, soaking up bullets and laying down suppressing fire.

TACTICAL — DOME SHIELD

Deploys a dome-shield that blocks attacks, active for 15 seconds. A versatile gadget that even gives you enough time to pick up downed allies.

ULTIMATE — BOMBARDMENT

Calls in a focused mortar strike on a marked position. The second you can use this in a firefight, do so: it deals massive damage and is hard to escape from.

Gibraltar's Ultimate has very good range: throw the device used to call in Bombardment as far as you can and see distant teams scramble for safety!

The Dome of Protection isn't a wall – don't get blindsided by enemies sneaking around it to take you by surprise.

Gibraltar players like shotguns: the shield that pops up when aiming down sights means close range encounters work better than long ones.

CLASS BREAKDOWN
LIFELINE

DEDICATED, UNCOMPROMISING AND INTELLIGENT, LIFELINE IS ALWAYS AT THE CRUX OF AN APEX TEAM THAT WORKS TOGETHER.

Of all the people battling it out in the Apex Games, Ajay Che (alias: Lifeline) is perhaps the most unlikely. The selfless combat medic was appalled to learn that her parents were incredibly wealthy war profiteers, and moved away as soon as she discovered the horrors they helped enable.

She soon enlisted in the Frontier Corps: a humanitarian outfit that prides itself on helping out communities in peril. Not content with saving lives on the front lines as a medic, Lifeline joined the Apex Games with hopes of securing more funding for the Corps.

Despite that sarcastic, nonchalant persona, Lifeline is a deeply caring person whose every act is selfless and fuelled by kindness. Lifeline knows her actions in the Games cost lives, but to her the ends justify the means: her winnings will save more people than she eliminates.

PASSIVE

COMBAT MEDIC

Revive knocked down teammates faster while protected by a shield wall. Also, all healing items are used 25% faster – meaning you can outheal wounded enemies.

TACTICAL

D.O.C. HEAL DRONE

Call your Drone of Compassion to automatically heal nearby teammates over time. Though it has small range, it helps conserve healing items.

ULTIMATE

CARE POD

Calls in a drop pod full of high-quality defensive gear. Upside: potential for very good armour. Downside: calls attention to your location.

Stick with your team: Lifeline is best used in group situations and most of her abilities are useless if you're out on your own.

Care Packages are loud. You can use one as bait to disguise your movements when you know enemies are approaching your location.

Be attentive: The boosted revives you get mean you can outspeed enemy teams in dogfights – and this can be vital.

MIRAGE

COCKY, TRICKY AND ALWAYS WITH SOMETHING TO SAY, MIRAGE IS KNOWN FOR HIS CONFIDENCE SCAMS AND HOLOGRAPHIC DECEPTION.

Anyone who knows Mirage has probably heard him say something like "I don't take myself too seriously. I don't take myself anywhere. I need to get out more,'' and that, really, is everything you need to know about him.

Mirage is the kind of person that likes attention – for all eyes to be on him. After his brothers went missing during the Frontier War, Mirage put the training he'd been doing all his life to use. He developed the tech his mother created for Holo-Pilots and made it better.

After spending a few years working in bars, listening to the locals talk up how good the Apex Games are, Mirage decided to enter (with his mother's blessing!). She even gave him the Holo-tech she'd been working on her whole career. Awh, bless.

Mirage now lives his best life, charming audiences and cheating opponents in the Apex Games.

PASSIVE

ENCORE!

Automatically drop a decoy and cloak for five seconds when knocked down. Not the best passive, but allows for quick pick-ups if the enemy isn't paying attention.

TACTICAL

PSYCHE OUT

Send out a holographic decoy to confuse the enemy. This is best used to distract and disorientate enemies – fake out a push then flank them.

ULTIMATE

VANISHING ACT

Deploy a team of Decoys to distract enemies while you cloak. A really good late game Ultimate, since it crowds the smaller rings and gives you a heads-up.

Mirage belongs on the front line. Get into the middle of the action, set up attacks and draw out foes with the hologram.

The Ultimate is versatile and can be used to either escape unwinnable fights, or put pressure on weakened teams.

Enemies reveal their location when they shoot Mirage's holograms. Poke fights to draw enemies out, then orchestrate team kills to finish them off.

CLASS BREAKDOWN

OCTANE

A THRILL-SEEKING ADRENALINE JUNKIE WITH A TASTE FOR EXPLOSIVES, OCTANE BRINGS A WARPED SENSE OF FUN TO THE APEX GAMES.

Octavio Silva is the son of the preoccupied CEOs of Silva Pharmaceuticals – and he gets bored. He gets so bored, so often. Thanks to the privileged background he grew up in, Silva often found himself wanting for nothing in life. So, to help address his chronic boredom, he would make daredevil videos and upload them for his myriad fans to enjoy across the planets.

One day, he had the bright idea of launching himself across the finish line with a grenade. It... didn't go as planned. The doctors amputated his legs and told him his days of being a stuntman were over. Instead, Silva enlisted the help of an old friend – Ajay Che, better known as Lifeline – and pressured her into replacing his broken legs with shiny new bionic ones.

Now able to repair his legs on the fly, Silva could chase bigger rushes than just silly stunts: he could enter the Apex Games and kill his boredom for good.

PASSIVE — SWIFT MEND

Automatically restores health over time. You regain one health every two seconds when not taking damage. It has great synergy with Stim, so don't be stingy with it.

TACTICAL — STIM

Move 30% faster for six seconds, but costs health to use. This is a great game starting utility: Stimming after the jump gets you a head start on looting.

ULTIMATE — LAUNCH PAD

Deploy a jump pad that catapults teammates through the air. Really handy when trying to disengage from persistent foes or reach higher ground.

Launch Pads are best used before engaging with enemies, rather than mid-battle. Make sure your team knows where the escape route is!

Playing Octane properly means you'll often get pinned by multiple enemies. Use Stim to speed up and get out. Then come back for more.

Octane is quick and can be hard to hit – use that risk/reward to your advantage and distract enemies as your allies set up kills.

PATHFINDER

PLAYFUL, UPBEAT AND ALWAYS HAPPY TO HELP, PATHFINDER IS THE MOST WHOLESOME PRESENCE IN THE APEX GAMES.

Pathfinder is a MRVN (Mobile Robotic Versatile eNtity) who has been modified to specialise in surveying the environment and scouting the often uncharted lands ahead of missions in the Outlands. Rumours have it that the friendly robot booted up decades ago in an abandoned laboratory – he had no idea who created him, or indeed why he was created.

With only his MRVN designation to hint at his identity, Pathfinder set off to do what he is so good at doing: scouting. Scouting for his creator. Since he began his journey, Pathfinder has learned a lot. He's learned a lot about food (his favourite dish to make is the Eastern Leviathan Stew), but he's still at a loss as to who made him.

Pathfinder is canny. He knows that if he can gain enough notoriety in the Apex Games, he can perhaps get famous enough to draw the attention of his creator back onto him.

PASSIVE

INSIDER KNOWLEDGE

Scan a survey beacon to reveal the ring's next location – a very useful ability if you want to get ahead of the game and start laying traps for incoming players.

TACTICAL

GRAPPLING HOOK

Grapple to get to out-of-reach places quickly. Used to flee enemies and navigate around the map, and useful for staying out of sight until you're ready to engage.

ULTIMATE

ZIPLINE GUN

Keep an eye out for players that stray from their teams. Pathfinder can use this Ultimate to flank and outmanoeuvre them, ideal for picking off loners.

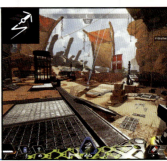

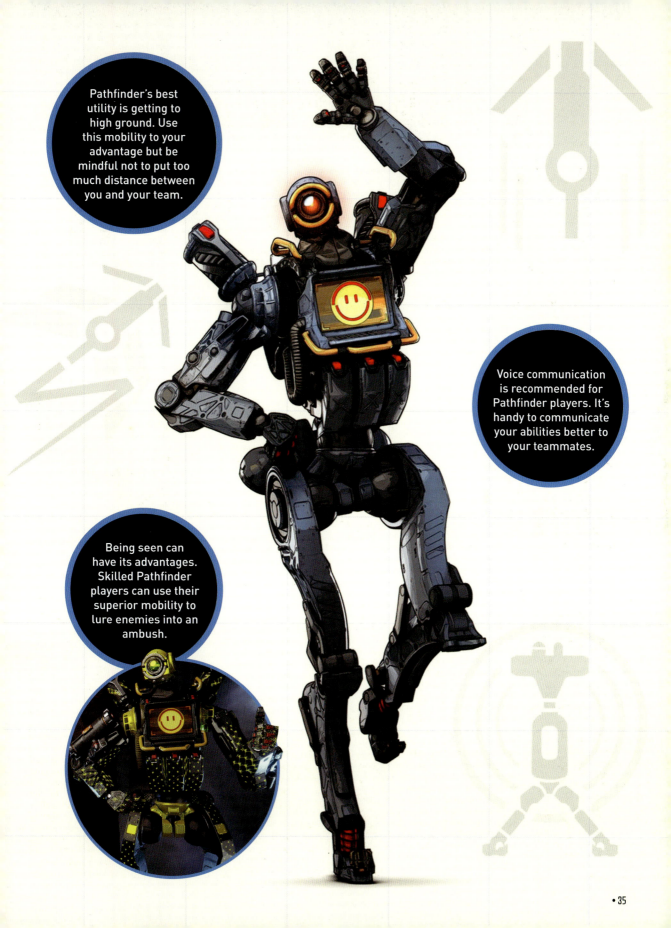

Pathfinder's best utility is getting to high ground. Use this mobility to your advantage but be mindful not to put too much distance between you and your team.

Voice communication is recommended for Pathfinder players. It's handy to communicate your abilities better to your teammates.

Being seen can have its advantages. Skilled Pathfinder players can use their superior mobility to lure enemies into an ambush.

WRAITH

INTERDIMENSIONAL SKIRMISHER WRAITH IS A TROUBLED BUT EXCELLENT WARRIOR, PLAGUED BY HER PAST BUT SET ON HER FUTURE.

Wraith has a command of the battlefield that other combatants can only dream of: the terrifying ability to rend space and time and open rifts in reality. This makes her a whirlwind fighter, a rapid, unpredictable enemy... but she has no idea how she gained these powers.

Wraith woke up in an IMC Detention Facility for the mentally ill years ago – and she remembered nothing. She had no clue how she got to where she was, or what her life had been before. The only thing she knew was the distant voice whispering in her mind, the voice that would starve her of sleep and challenge her sanity.

Determined to uncover her true identity, Wraith learned to listen to the voice, and it started to tell her how to use her odd powers. The facilities that were used to experiment on her are buried under the Apex Games arenas... so now Wraith is here, with a score to settle.

PASSIVE — VOICES FROM THE VOID

A voice warns you when danger approaches. As far as you can tell, it's on your side. Effective in solo play and groups – as long as you communicate!

TACTICAL — INTO THE VOID

Reposition quickly through the safety of void space, avoiding all damage. This is a handy ability to use to sneak up and assassinate enemies with.

ULTIMATE — DIMENSIONAL RIFT

Link two locations with portals for 60 seconds, allowing your entire team to use them. You're left vulnerable, but it can help get teammates out of bad situations.

Lots of clutch plays come down to Wraith's ability to teleport and escape: she's a late-game hero. Watch out for enemy Wraiths when it gets down to the final few squads.

Wraith is best put to use for situational awareness: sneaking around and highlighting enemies for your team should be a priority.

When attacking enemies at long to medium range, set up a portal for your team to escape through. This aids regrouping, and draws out attackers too.

BUILDING THE PERFECT SQUAD

APEX LEGENDS' HEROES MAKE IT UNIQUE, AND MASTERING HOW
THEY ALL WORK TOGETHER IS VITAL TO YOUR VICTORY.

SNEAKY SMOKE AND SIGHT

BLOODHOUND, BANGALORE, WRAITH

By leveraging one of the most powerful tactical abilities in the game (Lifeline's smoke grenade) with a player that can see through smoke (Bloodhound), you can theoretically wipe out entire teams without even being detected. Use Wraith to portal up and send Bloodhound in and you're onto a winner.

THE OL' BAIT & SWITCH

GIBRALTAR, MIRAGE, WRAITH

By utilising Gibraltar's Tactical bubble shield and Wraith's Ultimate portal, you can lead enemy teams into a dangerous situation. They'll come to the bubble, expecting to pressure you and find it empty. Then you can come around on them, pop Mirage's Ultimate to disorientate them more, and punish.

PURE AGGRESSION

BLOODHOUND, PATHFINDER, BANGALORE

If you want to get in the thick of the action, this is the team for you. Smart players can use Bloodhound to track enemies and intercept them, Pathfinder players can create quick routes to where they're headed, and Bangalore can smoke them before they know what's happening. Play it smart, and play two steps ahead.

TROJAN HORSE

GIBRALTAR, LIFELINE, CAUSTIC

A team for more passive players. If you consistently get to the end game and fall down there, this may be for you. Use Lifeline to heal up allies in Gibraltar's shield and use Caustic's gas to keep enemies at bay. The shield can also be useful when Lifeline calls in packages to make sure you don't get rushed.

THE SPEEDRUNNERS

OCTANE, WRAITH, MIRAGE

This is a team that causes headaches for enemies: Wraith, Octane and Mirage are all tricky to pin down and fire on. Keep escaping and breaking the enemy's line of sight. Consider baiting enemy teams into each other and picking off the survivors, coaxing them out with Mirage's holograms.

THE SURVIVALISTS

PATHFINDER, BLOODHOUND, MIRAGE

This build focuses on outliving other teams by avoiding the frontlines. Pathfinder's Passive tells you where the next ring will be, so you can head in and use Bloodhound's tracker to avoid other teams. Mirage's Ultimate should buy you time if you get spotted. Pilfer, loot and get the best items until you're forced to fight.

RING CLOSING

YOU ARE THE

CHAMPION

ItsKorvyy

PINGS

THE PING SYSTEM HELPS SET APEX LEGENDS APART FROM ITS PEERS. IT'S A UNIQUE MECHANIC, AND ONE THAT TAKES TIME TO MASTER.

Apex Legends immediately stood out from the battle royale crowd by introducing the 'Ping' system to the game. Mapped to the right bumper on consoles and to the mouse wheel on PC, the Ping system is an ingenious way that players can call attention to items in-game – even without using voice chat. By including a system like this in battle royale game, Respawn has effectively lowered the barrier of entry for the title, revolutionising the whole genre.

Pings cover many actions, from marking enemies to announcing the location of loot bins, calling 'dibs' on distant booty to telling teammates where you want the team to travel to.

Pinging not only calls attention to something in-game via a dedicated voice line from your character, it'll also pop a text message in the chat and mark a location on your teammates' HUD – both super simple features that are incredibly valuable in practice. Never forget to ping: it can be the difference between life and death.

ATTACKING HERE

DEFENDING THIS AREA

ENEMY

GO / GOING HERE

LOOTING HERE

SOMEONE'S BEEN HERE

WATCHING HERE

DO
Respond to other players' pings. How will your allies know you've acknowledged their location suggestion if you don't respond? Be polite.

DO
Ping from your inventory. If you need more of any specific ammo, you can hover over it in your screen and hit the ping button. Don't be afraid to ask.

DO
Ping enemy locations. All the time. Even if they're as far away as can be. Having that blip on the map could save your life one day.

DO
Ping loot caches, even in the late game. You never know who's less decked out than you and may need that Blue Helmet, even in round four!

DON'T
Spam pings. It's all well and good repeatedly pinging 'Mozambique here', but doing it while an ally is listening for enemy steps could cost you the game.

DON'T
Horde items. If your teammate is requesting shields or health, you can drop them from your inventory. Three players are always better than two.

DON'T
Forget to ping when you're knocked down. A downed player has good eyes on the action and you pinging an enemy's location could save a life.

DON'T
Forget to cancel. Pings can interfere with a player's HUD, and a forgotten location ping on-screen could be a crucial distraction that proves fatal.

REVIVING & RESPAWNING

LEARN HOW TO BRING YOUR TEAM BACK FROM THE JAWS OF DEFEAT, AND YOU'LL BE THE BEST APEX LEGENDS COMEBACK KID THERE EVER WAS.

KNOW HOW TO REVIVE

Apex Legends is unique in battle royale games thanks to its respawn mechanic. To bring allies back, you'll need to recover their banner from the loot box they drop when they die, then head to a Respawn Beacon. A drop ship will soon come and deliver your ally back into the game.

BE A GOOD DOWNED ALLY

If you die, you'll be able to watch the camera of one of your teammates, or hang around your dropped banner for a while. Here, you can act as a lookout, speaking to your teammates and letting them know the locations of incoming threats.

GET YOURSELF UP!

If you're lucky enough to find a Gold tier (level 4) backpack out in the wild, you'll gain the ability to self-revive. This takes a little while to charge, but can be a very handy form of deceit when you get knocked, scramble to safety and ambush an unsuspecting enemy.

KNOW YOUR TIMES

The first time you get knocked down in a game, it will take you 90 seconds to bleed out. The second time you get knocked down, it will reduce to 60 seconds. Respawning at a Beacon will reset these times – always remember that!

FIDDLE WITH THE HUD

When a teammate is knocked down or killed, an icon will appear on your HUD: Red for knocked, green for eliminated. These big icons can be a pain – you can head to Settings, then Gameplay tab, then set Ping Opacity to Faded to make this a bit less intrusive when you're playing.

DON'T FORGET TO SHARE

Respawned teammates come back with no gear at all. If it's late game, try and locate nearby death boxes brimming with loot. Alternatively, don't be afraid to drop your own guns: two players with a weapon each is better than a fully naked, vulnerable player.

BE QUICK OR BE DEAD

A downed ally's banner only hangs around for about 90 seconds once they've been killed, so either make a dash to get their banner or they'll be out of the game entirely. Sometimes risking it to grab their banner and revive them is worth it!

LOOTING

LIKE ANY BATTLE ROYALE, SUCCESS IN APEX LEGENDS CAN HINGE ON WHAT — AND HOW — YOU LOOT.

LOOT TIERS

To understand the best items to loot and pick up, you need to know what you're looking for. First of all, here are the different tiers of loot in Apex Legends.

 COMMON   EPIC

 RARE   LEGENDARY

LOOT TICKS

Hidden across the maps – spawning in different places in different matches – you'll find Loot Ticks. These are identical to the Apex Crates you'll open from the main menu, and are often found in built-up locations.

Listen out when you're looting areas with buildings. You can hear them bleeping and blooping, so make sure to sniff around corners and on top of platforms if you hear some strange robotic noises.

WHAT TO LOOK FOR

With any loot, you're going to want to look for the best colours. Gold Legendary items give you top-tier stats, as well as bonus benefits. The earlier you get these items, the better your chance of survival.

HIGH PRIORITY!

Occasionally, you'll find 'gold' versions of weapons that come fully equipped with best-in-class attachments. Usually found in Hot Zones, these weapons will massively improve your chances in the early- to mid-game.

DON'T BE SELFISH

Apex Legends is a team game, so you don't need to take everything yourself. Remember to ping your teammates with loot locations – you never know who's going to be more effective with any given loot item than you are.

LOOT TYPES

There are a lot of different types of loot to find in the game. Breaking them down into different categories is vital if you want to best understand how to take advantage of them.

WEAPON ATTACHMENTS

SNIPER STOCK
Improves the sniper's handling speed and idle sway

STANDARD STOCK
Improves rifle or SMG handling speed and idle sway

EXTENDED LIGHT MAG
Increases ammo size for light guns

EXTENDED HEAVY MAG
Increases ammo size for heavy guns

HOP-UPS
Changes how a weapon operates and works

BARREL STABILIZERS
Decreases recoil for many different weapons

SHOTGUN BOLT
Increases shotgun fire-rate

OPTICS

Digital Threat:
Highlights enemies
Digital Sniper Threat: Highlights enemies, Variable zoom

3x HCOG 'Ranger':
Variable zoom. For Snipers, LMGs, ARs, SMGs

2x-4x Variable AOG: Variable zoom. For Snipers, LMGs, ARs, SMGs

4x-8x Variable Sniper: Variable zoom. For Snipers

2x HCOG 'Bruiser':
For all guns

6x Sniper: For Snipers

1x-2x Variable Holo: Variable zoom. All guns

1x Holo: All guns

1x HCOG 'Classic': All guns

ARMOUR

Body Shield (Level 4)
+100 Shield Capacity. Full shield recharge when you execute knocked enemies

Helmet (Level 4)
25% damage reduction. Increases Tactical, Ultimate recharge speed

Knockdown Shield (Level 4)
750 Health Knockdown Shield. Allows self-revive on knockdown

Backpack (Level 4)
Adds 6 inventory slots. Doubles speed of healing items

Body Shield (Level 3)
+100 Shield Capacity

Helmet (Level 3)
25% damage reduction

Knockdown Shield (Level 3)
750 Health Knockdown Shield

Backpack (Level 3)
Adds 6 inventory slots

Body Shield (Level 2)
+75 Shield Capacity

Helmet (Level 2)
20% damage reduction

Knockdown Shield (Level 2)
250 Health Knockdown Shield

Backpack (Level 2)
Adds 4 inventory slots

Body Shield (Level 1)
+50 Shield Capacity

Helmet (Level 1)
10% damage reduction

Knockdown Shield (Level 1)
100 Health Knockdown Shield

Backpack (Level 1)
Adds 2 inventory slots

PISTOLS

THE MOST VERSATILE GUNS IN THE GAME ARE ALSO THE EASIEST TO FIND.

Pistols are notable for their handling: if you're a mobile, quick player try and master the Wingman. It goes well with good Octane, Mirage and Pathfinder players.

WINGMAN

The most powerful and popular gun in the early days of Apex Legends, the Wingman is every run-and-gunner's best friend. Modelled on a classic revolver, the handgun can take down opponents in three shots (if you've got a good aim) and if you can handle the weighty kick, it can carry you to victory every time.

AMMO TYPE	MAG SIZE	DPS
HEAVY	DEFAULT: 6 / LEVEL 3: 12	[BODY] 45 / [HEAD] 90
PROS		CONS
CAN QUICKLY TAKE OUT ENEMIES IN THE EARLY GAME		KICKS LIKE A MULE
HEADSHOTS PACK A LETHAL PUNCH		APPALLING ACCURACY FROM THE HIP

TOP ATTACHMENT

SKULLPIERCER RIFLING

INCREASES HEADSHOT DAMAGE BY OVER 2X

TOP ATTACHMENT

DIGITAL THREAT

RE-45

AMMO TYPE	MAG SIZE	DPS
LIGHT	DEFAULT 15 / LEVEL 3: 24	[BODY] 11 / [HEAD] 16
PROS		CONS
TIGHT BULLET SPREAD, EASY TO FOCUS FIRE		SMALL MAGAZINE, QUICKLY NEED TO RELOAD
QUICK AND MOBILE HANDLING		QUICKLY OUTCLASSED BY HIGHER-TIER GUNS

P2020

AMMO TYPE	MAG SIZE	DPS
LIGHT	DEFAULT: 10 / LEVEL 3: 18	[BODY] 12 / [HEAD] 18
PROS		CONS
TIGHT, PREDICTABLE BULLET SPREAD		LOW OVERALL DAMAGE OUTPUT
GOOD FOR HOLDING WEAPON ATTACHMENTS		SEMI-AUTOMATIC IS OUTCLASSED BY FULL AUTOMATIC WEAPONS

SHOTGUNS

CLOSE-RANGE EXPERTS AND TRAP LAYERS – SHOTGUNS ARE YOUR BEST ALLIES.

MASTIFF

A legendary shotgun only found in airdrops, there's a reason this weapon only comes with 20 ammo pre-loaded. The semi-automatic monster can chew through even Legendary-tier body armour with ease. If you see an enemy with this, engage from afar.

AMMO TYPE	MAG SIZE	DPS
UNIQUE	DEFAULT: 4	[BODY] UP TO 188 / [HEAD] UP TO 288V
PROS		CONS
CAN PRETTY MUCH ONE-SHOT FOES, EARLY- TO MID-GAME		VERY SMALL AMMO CLIP
NEGLIGIBLE RECOIL MAKES IT EASY TO USE		ONE OF THE RAREST GUNS IN THE GAME

TOP ATTACHMENT
DIGITAL THREAT

MOZAMBIQUE

AMMO TYPE	MAG SIZE	DPS
SHOTGUN	DEFAULT 3	[BODY] UP TO 45 / [HEAD] UP TO 66
PROS		CONS
RELATIVELY FAST RATE OF FIRE		APPALLING DAMAGE OUTPUT FOR SHOTGUN CLASS
QUICK, RESPONSIVE HANDLING		TERRIBLE MAGAZINE SIZE

TOP ATTACHMENT
PRECISION CHOKE

PEACEKEEPER

AMMO TYPE	MAG SIZE	DPS
SHOTGUN	DEFAULT: 6	[BODY] UP TO 110 / [HEAD] UP TO 165
PROS		CONS
VERY HIGH DAMAGE OUTPUT IF ALL BULLETS HIT		BASE WEAPON HAS LOW RATE OF FIRE
EVEN DEADLIER WITH PRECISION CHOKE		LIMITED MAGAZINE SIZE

TOP ATTACHMENT
LEGENDARY SHOTGUN BOLT

EVA-8 AUTO

AMMO TYPE	MAG SIZE	DPS
SHOTGUN	DEFAULT 8	[BODY] UP TO 63 / [HEAD] UP TO 90
PROS		CONS
HIGH DAMAGE POTENTIAL		UNPREDICTABLE BULLET SPREAD
DEADLY IN PRACTISED HANDS		NOT VERY CUSTOMISABLE

FIRING RANGE

SMGs

IF YOU WANT TO SUPPRESS CLOSE-RANGE ENEMIES, SMGs ARE FOR YOU.

R-99

The R-99 will most likely be one of the first weapons you pick up after you drop, and something you'll at least take until the mid-game. It's reliable, customisable and provides decent damage output from close- to mid-range. Learn to use this weapon, and you'll be able to survive the early-game feeding frenzy with ease.

TOP ATTACHMENT
LEGENDARY BARREL STABILISER

A good SMG player will prioritise upgrading the magazine: you can dish out pretty good damage per second with SMGs, but only if you have enough bullets!

AMMO TYPE	MAG SIZE	DPS
LIGHT	DEFAULT: 18 / LEVEL 3: 30	[BODY] 12 / [HEAD] 18
PROS		CONS
RAPID RATE OF FIRE		LOWEST DAMAGE OF ALL SMG CLASS GUNS
HIGH MAGAZINE CAPACITY		NEEDS ATTACHMENTS TO BE *REALLY* GOOD

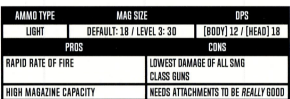

TOP ATTACHMENT
SELECTFIRE RECEIVER

PROWLER BURST PDW

AMMO TYPE	MAG SIZE	DPS
HEAVY	DEFAULT: 20 / LEVEL 3: 35	[BODY] UP TO 70 PER BURST / [HEAD] UP TO 105 PER BURST
PROS		CONS
WITH FULLY AUTOMATIC FIRE, CAN DEAL GREAT DAMAGE		BURST FIRE ISN'T AMAZING, NEEDS HOP-UP TO BE VALID
SUITS VARIETY OF PLAYSTYLES		RECOIL IS VERY HARD TO MASTER

TOP ATTACHMENT
DIGITAL THREAT

ALTERNATOR SMG

AMMO TYPE	MAG SIZE	DPS
LIGHT	DEFAULT: 16 / LEVEL 3: 26	[BODY] 13 / [HEAD] 19
PROS		CONS
SMALL, LIGHT, EASY TO USE		LOW DAMAGE OUTPUT
PREDICTABLE VERTICAL RECOIL PATTERN		USELESS WITHOUT MULTIPLE ATTACHMENTS

LMGs

IN THE RIGHT HANDS, LMGs CAN TAKE DOWN AN ENTIRE TEAM.

M600 SPITFIRE

TOP ATTACHMENT
LEGENDARY BARREL STABILISER

The whole LMG class can lay down big damage – but at the cost of mobility. Though both guns are particularly dangerous, the Spitfire edges out on top of the Devotion because of its massive damage per shot, huge Level 3 magazine size and ferocity at more or less every range.

AMMO TYPE	MAG SIZE	DPS
LIGHT	DEFAULT: 35 / LEVEL 3: 60	[BODY] 20 / [HEAD] 40
PROS		CONS
VERY HIGH DAMAGE PER SHOT		SLOW TO RELOAD AND READY UP
VERY HIGH MAGAZINE CAPACITY		FIRE RATE CHUGS – NOT IDEAL WITH ZIGZAG RECOIL

TOP ATTACHMENT
TURBOCHARGER

DEVOTION

AMMO TYPE	MAG SIZE	DPS
ENERGY	DEFAULT: 44: 6	[BODY] 17 / [HEAD] 34
PROS		CONS
ONCE THE 'SPIN-UP' KICKS IN, LAYS DOWN BIG DAMAGE		VERY LONG RELOAD ANIMATION
LARGE MAGAZINE ALLOWS GUN TO WIPE OUT WHOLE TEAMS		RPM ACCELERATION CAN COST YOU YOUR LIFE

If you want to master LMGs, be sure to always keep context in mind. A Devotion dressed up with a Turbocharger can quickly put entire enemy teams to bed in the smaller rings, whereas a Spitfire with a big magazine can be a very handy gun to keep enemies at bay as you beat a tactical retreat.

ARs

EASY TO USE, EASY TO FIND AND EASY TO MASTER – AN IDEAL WEAPON CLASS FOR BEGINNERS.

R-301

TOP ATTACHMENT
EPIC EXTENDED LIGHT MAG

This gun, which can be found everywhere in the game, is a good all-purpose option in Apex Legends. Fuelled up with the most common ammo in the game, and laying down double the damage with a headshot, this gun is a perfect all-rounder and will be useful even when you're down to the final few teams.

AMMO TYPE	MAG SIZE	DPS
LIGHT	DEFAULT: 18 / LEVEL 3: 28	[BODY] 14 / [HEAD] 28
PROS		CONS
HIGH ACCURACY AND HIGH RATE OF FIRE		LOW BASE DAMAGE
ONE OF THE BEST LONG-RANGE RIFLES		LOW BASE MAGAZINE SIZE

TOP ATTACHMENT
EPIC EXTENDED HEAVY MAG

VK-47 FLATLINE

AMMO TYPE	MAG SIZE	DPS
HEAVY	DEFAULT: 20 / LEVEL 3: 30	[BODY] 16 / [HEAD] 32
PROS		CONS
HIGH BASE DAMAGE, DOUBLED ON HEADSHOT		POOR ACCURACY AND HIGH, UNPREDICTABLE RECOIL
GREAT AT CLOSE AND MEDIUM RANGE		USELESS AT LONG RANGE

TOP ATTACHMENT
EPIC EXTENDED HEAVY MAG

HEMLOCK BURST AR

AMMO TYPE	MAG SIZE	DPS
HEAVY	DEFAULT: 18 / LEVEL	[BODY] 18 / [HEAD] 36
PROS		CONS
HIGH ACCURACY, AND GREAT DAMAGE IF ALL THREE BULLETS HIT		LOW BASE RATE OF FIRE AND MAGAZINE CAPACITY
SATISFYING RATE OF FIRE AT MEDIUM TO LONG RANGE		POOR CHOICE FOR CLOSE-RANGE ENCOUNTERS

TOP ATTACHMENT
TURBOCHARGER

HAVOC RIFLE

AMMO TYPE	MAG SIZE	DPS
ENERGY	DEFAULT: 25	[BODY] 18 / [HEAD] 36
PROS		CONS
HIGH DAMAGE PER SECOND FOR AR CLASS		PRETTY HARD TO USE AND MASTER WITHOUT TURBOCHARGER
VERSATILE, GOOD FOR DIFFERENT CONTEXTS		RARE AMMO TYPE

SNIPERS

THERE'S NOTHING MORE SATISFYING THAN TAKING SOMEONE OUT FROM HALF A MAP AWAY.

KRABER

Though it can deliver a massive 250 headshot damage – capable of wiping out an opponent in one shot – this gun requires a dab hand to use properly. Landing in the game with only eight ammo, a masterful sniper can pick off whole enemy teams before they even know where you are. Just make sure you're quick, and accurate.

AMMO TYPE	MAG SIZE	DPS
UNIQUE	DEFAULT: 4	[BODY] 125 / [HEAD] 250
PROS		CONS
TOP-IN-GAME DAMAGE ON HEADSHOTS		COMES WITH PRECIOUS LITTLE AMMO
BODY SHOTS CAPABLE OF DOWNING UNDER-EQUIPPED ENEMIES		ONLY REALLY GEARED UP FOR LONG RANGE ENCOUNTERS

TOP ATTACHMENT

DIGITAL SNIPER THREAT

G7 SCOUT

AMMO TYPE	MAG SIZE	DPS
LIGHT	DEFAULT: 10 / LEVEL 3: 20	[BODY] 30 / [HEAD] 60
PROS		CONS
HIGHEST SNIPER RATE OF FIRE		WATCH OUT FOR THE GLOWING IRON SIGHT
GREAT FOR HEADSHOTS AND POTSHOTS AT RANGE		LOTS OF HARD, VERTICAL RECOIL

TOP ATTACHMENT

SKULLPIERCER RIFLING

LONGBOW DMR

AMMO TYPE	MAG SIZE	DPS
HEAVY	DEFAULT: 5 / LEVEL 3: 10	[BODY] 55 / [HEAD] 110
PROS		CONS
MASSIVE DAMAGE PER SHOT		TERRIBLE HIP FIRE ACCURACY AND PREDICTABILITY
CAN DOWN PRE-WOUNDED ENEMIES FROM AFAR		ATTACHMENTS DON'T CROP UP TOO OFTEN

TOP ATTACHMENT

PRECISION CHOKE

TRIPLE TAKE

AMMO TYPE	MAG SIZE	DPS
ENERGY	DEFAULT: 5	[BODY] 69 IF ALL HIT / [HEAD] 138 IF ALL HIT
PROS		CONS
THREE SHOTS WITH A TIGHT SPREAD MAKES IT HARD TO MISS		LOW MAGAZINE, CAN'T BE UPGRADED
IF ALL THREE BULLETS HIT, THERE'S GREAT DAMAGE POTENTIAL		NEEDS SKULLPIERCER TO LAY DOWN DECENT CRITICAL DAMAGE

TRAPS & STEALTH

SURVIVING AND OUTLASTING OTHER PLAYERS IN APEX IS KEY TO GETTING TO THE ENDGAME. AND WHEN YOU'RE THERE, YOU NEED TO PLAY DIRTY.

NOX NOX, WHO'S THERE?

PLAN

Caustic's Tactical Nox Grenades are solid items – they block doors. In places like Slums and Bunker, you can lock enemy teams in rooms and watch them suck up damage until they're doomed... a nasty play.

SET UP

Follow an enemy team into a tight area – this works anywhere with one or two doors sealing off a room. Keep your teammates on point to flank.

EXECUTE

If the whole team is in a room, pop your Tacticals down – two on each door. This will trap enemies in, if they crack a door or try to shoot their way out, they'll trigger the canisters. Try throwing down a grenade for good measure, too.

The best trapper in the game is Caustic. His Nox gas causes serious damage over time. If you spot a Caustic trap in the field, shoot the metal base to destroy it... just make sure you aim properly.

GET OVER HERE!

PLAN

Pathfinder's tactical Grapple can pull enemies in. So lay good guns or purple loot down on bridges in areas like the Swamps, where you can fall off the map, this is an unexpected play...

Head to an area where enemies can fall off the map: Runway, Swamps, anywhere at the edge of the map.

Bait another player with some enticing loot, then Grapple them from behind, sending them plummeting.

NOW YOU'RE THINKING WITH PORTALS

PLAN

Wraith's Ultimate portal is one of the most useful defensive utility abilities in the game – but this trick is a more aggressive use of the power.

SET UP

Get your whole team hidden in a room or small, enclosed area. Keep an eye on your flanks and head somewhere open and trigger your Ultimate.

EXECUTE

Run back to your team. If you know there's a target out there, wait behind the portal entrance. A disorientated enemy will emerge and get a back full of buckshot if all goes to plan. Sometimes even works for team wipes.

Different areas have different properties when it comes to movement and sound. Walking through water under wooden buildings is noisier than walking through grass, for example. The quicker you move, the more noise you make. The best Legends are silent.

SURVIVING THE ENDGAME

THIS IS WHAT YOU'VE BEEN TRAINING FOR: THE ONE ON ONES, THE CLUTCH PLAYS, THE MOMENTS OF GLORY. YOU GOT THIS.

The endgame is where Apex really comes into its own. It's where all elements of speed, ferocity, judgement and teamwork collide – leaving you in the smallest ring with nothing but one or two other teams keeping you from victory. It's tense, it's sweaty and it's hard – and it's easy to lose your head.

There are two schools of thought on the endgame: rushing and camping. Do you prefer to wait out the attacks of an oncoming team, or try and get the drop on them? All the heroes' abilities come into focus in these last few seconds, with some (Lifeline, Pathfinder) becoming less useful, as others (Mirage, Bangalore) become game-changing.

Examine your surroundings, know what healing items and projectiles you have on hand, and remember the strengths and weaknesses of the guns you're carrying. That should stand you in good enough stead to enter the fight and come out victorious.

DO

Flank. Outmanoeuvring enemies at this stage is vital. Use two players to draw out enemies, and the third can diverge and flank their position, often to devastating effect.

DO

Use your abilities. The action gets quicker when the ring is bearing down on you, but your abilities will still recharge. Late-game success requires risk to get reward, so pull out all the stops.

DO

Remember to loot death boxes. By the late game, recently downed players will have top tier loot: make sure to capitalise on this, take Phoenix Kits, recharge shields when possible.

DO

Use your throwables. Arc Stars, Thermite Grenades and Frags can be really good for cornering and weakening enemies. Block escape routes with Arcs and Thermite, and take some pot shots.

DON'T

Let the ring hem you in. Yes, in the later rounds it does do a lot of damage, but you can rush opponents from an angle they aren't expecting if you play smart and fast outside of the ring.

DON'T

Camp in buildings. Apex is a game that favours movement and speed – make sure you put pressure on the enemy, know where your next piece of cover is, and push for it when you can.

DON'T

Get pinned in low ground. If you are going to camp, then camp high and be vigilant. Don't let the appeal of gaining speed by sliding downhill get you cornered and trapped.

DON'T

Just rush in. It can be tempting to try and 'Leeroy Jenkins' the final seconds of a match, but that will only leave you and your team out of sync, out of cover and out of luck. Play it cool, until the end.

ADVANCED TIPS

THERE ARE A LOT OF LITTLE TRICKS IN APEX LEGENDS THAT WON'T BE IMMEDIATELY OBVIOUS. LET US FIX THAT FOR YOU.

Apex Legends is absolutely riddled with little character tips and quirks that you only really get to know about by playing a lot. It's a good job that we've been experimenting with this game more or less since it launched in order to sniff out some of the sneakiest, most vital pieces of information you wouldn't otherwise get to know.

Listed below is a rapid-fire list of some of the best bits of knowledge we've picked up over hundreds of hours of play. We hope it helps.

Octane's Tactical – Stim – will never take you below 1 health. If you're near death, you may as well be quick!

Doors take two kicks to break down, but if you time it with a teammate, you can knock them in 'one'. Good for ambushes.

Bloodhound can transform into his Ultimate immediately when on a zipline, meaning you can be combat ready if coming in hot.

You can slide backwards as quickly as you can slide forwards. Worth bearing in mind when you're retreating from incoming enemies.

Jump Kicking (jump then melee) has a quicker cooldown than regular melee, meaning you can chain more and do more damage by using this technique.

Caustic players should prioritise Thermite Grenades: the damage they do stacks with his Nox clouds to rapidly drain the health of anyone caught in both.

Wraith's portals block doors. Want to bide some time to heal, or create a diversion away from your allies? Wraith can surprise you.

Want a mobile bulletproof base? Deploy Lifeline's D.O.C., then pop Gibraltar's dome shield on top and voila! You can move it as you push forward.

Never aim down sights with shotguns: it takes time and they're cumbersome. Hipfire will usually have the same effect in less time.

Peacekeeper shotguns can be fired 'twice'. Fire, reload, switch weapon, then switch back. This whole cycle is quicker than reloading, and can devastate close-range enemies.

Wraith's portals last 60 seconds – but Respawn didn't include a timer... or did they? If you see 39% on your Ultimate charge, your portal is about to disappear.

Don't accidentally die by standing on confined supply bins as they open, or by standing under Supply Drops: both can squish you, bringing instant death.

Reloading while there is still ammo in your clip is faster than a 'full reload' on 90% of weapons in the game.

Generally speaking, it's better to swap out your Body Shield than heal up your current one. It saves time and keeps healing items in your inventory for when you might really need them.

If you have a Lifeline on your team, always give them the Ultimate Accelerant – it's the slowest charging Ult in the game and proffers the best rewards.

Finishers look good, but they're not practical. They don't all take the same amount of time, either: the shortest is four seconds and the longest is just over six.

SEASON 1 — WILD FRONTIER
BATTLE PASS

THE INAUGURAL SEASON OF APEX LEGENDS FEATURED A TON OF UPGRADES AND ITEMS TO COLLECT. CHECK OFF YOUR BATTLE PASS REWARDS HERE.

Apex Legends allows players to buy a Battle Pass every season, which grants access to 100 bonus rewards (on top of whatever you get out of Apex Packs).

As well as the 100 paid rewards, there are also 24 free rewards players can earn per season without paying for the Battle Pass. The rewards earned from the Battle Pass each season are exclusive, and won't be made available again after the season has ended, so if you want everything, you have to play a lot!

Each Battle Pass lasts about three months, but be aware that Respawn could change up timescales and pricing at any time in the future.

LEVEL	REWARD	FREE REWARD
1	Revolutionary Lifeline Skin, Outlaw Mirage Skin, Survivor Wraith Skin	–
2	Harvest Triple Take Skin	Apex Pack
3	Wraith Tracker – Season 1 Kills	–
4	Patchwork Hemlock Skin	Gibraltar Tracker – Season 1 Wins
5	Wild Frontier Level Badge	–
6	Opening Season Bangalore Quip	Pathfinder Tracker – Season 1 Wins
7	50 Apex Coins	–
8	Bloodhound Tracker – Season 1 Kills	Wraith Tracker – Season 1 Wins
9	Navigator Prowler Skin	–
10	Wild Frontier Level Badge	Bangalore Tracker – Season 1 Wins
11	50 Apex Coins	–
12	BP Point Boost: +5% survival time as BP per squad member.	Apex Pack
13	Funny Bones Mirage Frame	–
14	Navigator Longbow Skin	Bloodhound Tracker – Season 1 Wins
15	Wild Frontier Level Badge	–
16	Opening Season Mirage Quip	Caustic Tracker – Season 1 Wins

LEVEL	REWARD	FREE REWARD
17	50 Apex Coins	–
18	Flight Risk Octane Frame	Mirage Tracker – Season 1 Wins
19	Patchwork Spitfire Skin	–
20	Wild Frontier Level Badge	Lifeline Tracker – Season 1 Wins
21	50 Apex Coins	–
22	BP Point Boost: +2.5% survival time as BP per squad member.	Octane Tracker – Season 1 Wins
23	Silk Road Wraith Frame	–
24	Navigator Mozambique Skin	Apex Pack
25	Wild Frontier Level Badge	–

LEVEL	REWARD	FREE REWARD
26	Epic Apex Pack	Caustic Tracker – Season 1 Damage
27	Season Opening Pathfinder Quip	–
28	Mirage Tracker – Season 1 Kills	Bangalore Tracker – Season 1 Damage
29	Harvest Kraber Skin	–
30	Wild Frontier Level Badge	Gibraltar Tracker – Season 1 Damage
31	50 Apex Coins	–
32	BP Point Boost: +2.5% survival time as BP per squad member.	Bloodhound Tracker – Season 1 Damage
33	Pathfinder Tracker – Season 1 Kills	–
34	Patchwork EVA Skin	Apex Pack
35	Wild Frontier Level Badge	
36	Opening Season Caustic Quip	Lifeline Tracker – Season 1 Damage
37	50 Apex Coins	–
38	Caustic Tracker – Season 1 Kills	Octane Tracker – Season 1 Damage
39	Navigator Flatline Skin	–
40	Wild Frontier Level Badge	Wrath Tracker – Season 1 Damage
41	50 Apex Coins	–
42	BP Point Boost: +2.5% survival time as BP per squad member.	Mirage Tracker – Season 1 Damage
43	Apex Pack	–
44	Patchwork Alternator Skin	Pathfinder Tracker – Season 1 Damage
45	Wild Frontier Level Badge	–
46	Opening Season Gibraltar Quip	Apex Pack
47	50 Apex Coins	–
48	Gibraltar Tracker – Season 1 Kills	Messenger Octane Skin
49	Harvest Peacekeeper Skin	–
50	Wild Frontier Level Badge	–
51	Thrill of the Hunt Prowler Skin	–
52	BP Point Boost: +2.5% survival time as BP per squad member.	–
53	Apex Pack	–
54	Harvest Devotion Skin	–
55	Wild Frontier Level Badge	–
56	Opening Season Wraith Quip	–
57	100 Apex Coins	–
58	Octane Tracker – Season 1 Kills	–
59	Patchwork Mastiff Skin	–
60	Wild Frontier Level Badge	–

LEVEL	REWARD	FREE REWARD
61	Pick Me Up Lifeline Frame	–
62	BP Point Boost: +2.5% survival time as BP per squad member.	–
63	100 Apex Coins	–
64	Harvest P2020 Skin	–
65	Wild Frontier Level Badge	–
66	Opening Season Bloodhound Quip	–
67	100 Apex Coins	–
68	Lifeline Tracker – Season 1 Kills	–
69	Patchwork Havoc Skin	–
70	Wild Frontier Level Badge	–
71	Nock Down Bloodhound Frame	–
72	BP Point Boost: +2.5% survival time as BP per squad member.	–
73	Apex Pack	–
74	Harvest R99 Skin	–
75	Wild Frontier Level Badge	–
76	Open Season Octane Quip	–
77	100 Apex Coins	–
78	Bangalore Tracker – Season 1 Kills	–
79	Navigator Wingman Skin	–
80	Wild Frontier Level Badge	–
81	Land of Giants Gibraltar Frame	–
82	BP Point Boost: +2.5% survival time as BP per squad member.	–
83	Apex Pack	–
84	Patchwork RE-45 Skin	–
85	Wild Frontier Level Badge	–
86	Legendary Apex Pack	–
87	100 Apex Coins	–
88	Slaughterhouse Caustic Frame	–
89	BP Point Boost: +2.5% survival time as BP per squad member.	–
90	Wild Frontier Level Badge	–
91	Building Bridges Pathfinder Frame	–
92	BP Point Boost: +2.5% survival time as BP per squad member.	–
93	Apex Pack	–
94	Patchwork G7 Scout Skin	–
95	Wild Frontier Level Badge	–
96	Open Season Lifeline Quip	–
97	100 Apex Coins	–
98	Sharpened Senses Bangalore Frame	–
99	Harvest R-301 Skin	–
100	Wild Frontier Level Badge, The Silver Horn Havoc Skin, The Golden Idol Havoc Skin, Season 1 Badge	–

SECRETS & EASTER EGGS

APEX LEGENDS MAY SEEMS LIKE A PRETTY STRAIGHTFORWARD GAME AT FIRST GLANCE, BUT THERE'S A LOT GOING ON UNDER THE SURFACE...

NESSY!

Respawn managed to smuggle a cute Loch Ness Monster Easter egg into the game before the launch of the first season, hiding a secret encounter in the game if you find 10 little Nessy figures... and shoot them! Once you've managed to locate all the figures, you can travel to a specific spot on the map and see the creature make an in-game appearance.

TITANFALL REFERENCES

Apex Legends is set 30 years after the events of previous Respawn game, Titanfall 2. But that's not where the connections end. There's also a location in the map called Lastimosa Armory – anyone who has played Titanfall 2 will recognise this as a major character's name. Even Nessy made appearances in both previous Titanfall games.

HEIRLOOMS

There is a hidden set of items that have a 1% chance of dropping when you open an Apex Pack, known as the Apex Legends Heirloom Set. The set features a series of special items for Wraith, including:
- Knife Skin
- Intro Quip
- Banner Pose

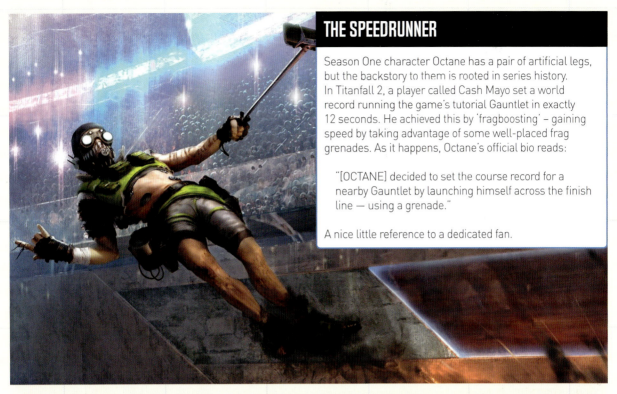

THE SPEEDRUNNER

Season One character Octane has a pair of artificial legs, but the backstory to them is rooted in series history. In Titanfall 2, a player called Cash Mayo set a world record running the game's tutorial Gauntlet in exactly 12 seconds. He achieved this by 'fragboosting' – gaining speed by taking advantage of some well-placed frag grenades. As it happens, Octane's official bio reads:

"[OCTANE] decided to set the course record for a nearby Gauntlet by launching himself across the finish line — using a grenade."

A nice little reference to a dedicated fan.

A RECURRING CHARACTER?

Bloodhound was not initially designed for Apex Legends. The all-seeing scout was originally meant to appear in a Titanfall game, according to an almost-complete render included in a Titanfall art book. But because the first Titanfall launched without a full story mode, it seems a lot of characters were cut.

Now Bloodhound lives – although sadly without the bow and arrow they were originally seen with. What other leftover design ideas and concepts never made it into Respawn's original games? We may never know.

STAY SAFE ONLINE

APEX LEGENDS IS ALL FUN AND GAMES — FOR THE MOST PART. IT'S ALSO AN ONLINE EXPERIENCE WITH OTHER PLAYERS, AND IT PAYS TO REMEMBER THAT.

Apex Legends is a hugely popular game – one that managed to attract a massive 50 million players within its first month online. Not all of those players are going to be as interested in making the game a safe, enjoyable space as you are, so there are a few things you should be aware of.

Though you can turn on Voice Chat for yourself, there is no way of permanently turning off voice chat for other players – you will have to manually mute them on a game-to-game basis if you want to turn off all incoming chat. Bear that in mind, if you find yourself in a loud team.

As of an update early on in the game's life, you can now report players too. If anything another player says is hateful, inappropriate, upsetting or threatening, then make sure to use this feature immediately and report that player to Respawn and EA.

DO

Report Players. If anything at all makes you feel uncomfortable, you can report players via the end-game screen by pressing the Right Stick in.

DO

Know your age rating. In the US, Apex Legends is rated 13+ and in the UK/EU it is rated 16+. These aren't legal restrictions, but they are recommended.

DO

Set up parental controls. There will be specific guides to setting up parental controls on Xbox One, PS4 and PC – see online to learn how to do this.

DO

Set your party to Private to prevent random players joining. This can be done from the Lobby, and helps you stick together with players you know.

DON'T

Be part of the problem. Toxic behaviour is prevalent in online gaming: don't make online spaces dangerous or unwelcoming to others.

DON'T

Give out personal information online. Never tell people where you live, give out bank information, or reveal personal knowledge to people you've never met.

DON'T

Spend money without permission. Apex Legends is free to download, but does include optional purchases – always get parental consent before buying.

DON'T

Forget to mute players. This can be done in the pre-game screens, or in-game via the menu. You don't have to listen to someone if you don't want to!

ACHIEVEMENT CHECKLIST

IF YOU NEED A LITTLE EXTRA INCENTIVE TO KEEP YOU PLAYING AND LEVELLING UP IN APEX LEGENDS, THERE ARE PLENTY OF ACHIEVEMENTS YOU CAN CHASE.

☐ **The Player – 100G / Silver**
Description: Reach player level 50.
Tips: Just keep playing!

☐ **Decked Out – 75G / Bronze**
Description: Equip a legendary Helmet and Body Armour at the same time.
Tips: Play with friends that are happy to drop items, let you equip, and give back.

☐ **Team Player – 75G / Bronze**
Description: Respawn a teammate.
Tips: Be attentive, always know where your nearest Respawn Point is, make sure to grab allies' Banners when possible.

☐ **Fully Kitted – 75G / Bronze**
Description: Equip a fully kitted weapon.
Tips: Equip a Legendary attachment in every slot of a weapon. Pistols are the easiest for this – they only have two slots.

☐ **Jumpmaster – 75G / Bronze**
Description: Be the Jumpmaster 5 times.
Tips: Just keep playing, and don't relinquish control, even if you're feeling under pressure!

☐ **Well-Rounded – 100G / Silver**
Description: Deal 5,000 damage with 8 different Legends.
Tips: Keep playing, and don't get too precious about any one hero. Make sure to rotate frequently.

☐ **Kill Leader – 75G / Bronze**
Description: Become the Kill Leader.
Tips: Try and capitalise on under-equipped enemies in the early game if you luck out with a good gun.

☐ **Apex Offense – 75G / Bronze**
Description: Win the game as an offensive character.
Tips: See Wraith, Bangalore, Octane and Mirage character pages.

☐ **Apex Defense – 75G / Bronze**
Description: Win the game as a defensive character.
Tips: See Gibraltar and Caustic character pages.

☐ **Apex Support – 75G / Bronze**
Description: Win the game as a support character.
Tips: See Pathfinder and Lifeline character pages.

☐ **Apex Recon – 75G / Bronze**
Description: Win the game as a recon character.
Tips: See Bloodhound character page.

☐ **Apex Legend – 125G / Gold**
Description: Win a game with 8 different Legends.
Tips: Keep playing, keep getting better, keep learning new tricks and keep mastering the systems and you'll get this eventually.